Attitude

To Change your Life,
Change your Attitude

Rosie Hamilton McGinty

Hamilton McGinty
Personal Development Consultants
2 Aldingbourne House
Aldingbourne Drive
Crockerhill
Chichester
West Sussex
PO18 OLG

E Mail: rhamiltonm@AOL.com

ISBN 1 84024 110 1

Printed and bound by Caledonian International Book
Manufacturers, Glasgow.

To my two sons Andy and Matt
who have been 'the light of my life'.

Introduction

The Code of Emotional Literacy

The basis of one's character is Self-discipline, the virtuous life - based on self-control. Strength of character is being able to motivate and guide oneself, whether in doing work, finishing a job or getting up in the morning. We need to be in control of ourselves, our appetites, our passions and to do right by others. It takes WILL to keep emotion under the control of reason. Being able to put aside one's self-centred focus and impulses has social benefits: It opens the way to empathy, to real listening, to taking another person's perspective. Empathy leads to caring and compassion. Seeing things from another's perspective breeds tolerance and acceptance. In this sense emotional literacy goes hand in hand with education for character, for moral development and citizenship.

Develop Good Character Ethics

Character ethics:
A set of moral principals — a
personal code of right
conduct. Always do what is
morally and ethically correct,
it keeps your conscious clear.

Enthusiasm

A positive attitude
attracts others —
always demonstrate
enthusiasm in whatever you
say and do.

Pride

When you
respect yourself
others will respect you.
Take pride in your
individuality.

Honesty

Be trustworthy.
Start by being honest
with yourself.

Fidelity

Faithfulness and Loyalty.
Build solid foundations in
your relationships through
good communication.
Learn to share your
problems.

Courage

Ability to control or
suppress fear.
Turn fear into faith
and go forward.

Integrity

Honesty and Wholeness.
Develop a character
based on love and
compassion. Integrity cannot
be purchased, develop it now.

Modesty

Unpretentious.
Develop self-confidence
and drop the ego.
Be proud of
who you are.

Humility

Manners - humble attitude
of mind. Develop courtesy
and modesty in your
dealings with others.

Justice

Fairness - exercise authority.
Trust that justice goes with
truth.

Industry

Diligence - business activity.
The more effort you
put into your work the
more rewards you reap.

Simplicity

The fact or quality
of something simple.
Go back to basic living.

Intuition

Listen to your intuition.
Trust yourself and
your perceptions.
Have faith and confidence
in what you feel.

Happiness

When you get up in the
morning you have two
choices: to be happy or
unhappy. The happiness habit
is developed simply by
practising 'happy thinking'.

Forgiveness

Forgive - but learn
from the experience.

Trust

You can only trust
others when you
fully trust yourself.

Wealth

When you have
good health,
you have great wealth!

Anger

Feelings of extreme
displeasure. Develop
willpower to control negative
emotional feelings.

Envy

Jealousy and
discontent with
what one has.
Don't envy anyone
– wish them well.

Greed

Excessive desire for
food or wealth.
Develop self-discipline
and self-control,
find a balance.

Lust

Intense desire
for something
– usually short lived.
Learn to balance your
desires with
other interests.

Laziness

Develop motivation
and a positive attitude.
Help yourself
– by developing your
talents and skills.

Boost Your Self-esteem

Self-esteem is how you see yourself as a person. If you value the type of person you are — you have good self-esteem - you are proud to be you. People with good self-esteem respect others as well as themselves.

Good self-esteem.
Feeling good about yourself
enables you to be the person
you want to be and enjoy
others more fully – offer
more of yourself to the
world.

Low self-esteem can create a vicious cycle - lack of self confidence, unhappy personal life, poor performance, distorted view of self and others. People with low self-esteem put themselves down, fear failure, take the easy way out, resist change. Learn to be responsible and make necessary changes.

Make light of criticism - it
stems from insecurity.

If a situation is beyond
reconciliation, distance
yourself to regain your self-
esteem.

Whatever your level of self-esteem, take positive steps to improve it. Start by being honest with yourself. Develop a positive attitude by giving yourself: Acceptance – recognise strengths and weaknesses. Encouragement – take an "I can do it" attitude. Praise – take pride in your achievements. Trust – do what makes you feel happy and fulfilled. Respect – be proud of who you are. You can improve your self-esteem, it's really worth the effort.

I have valuable
skills and talents.
I respect my intelligence.
I act on my feelings
and beliefs.
I like my appearance.
I am worth knowing.
Basically
– I like who I am.

Develop A Positive Mental Attitude

Your attitude is important because it's the state of mind in which you approach a situation – it is the same you – the only difference is your attitude, which only YOU can control.

It's not enough to know the difference between a good and bad attitude, you've got to put your knowledge into action. It's up to you – you're the one who determines your attitude – in the way you look, what you say and the way you behave.

When you arise say out loud:
"I believe this is going to be a
wonderful day. I believe I can
successfully handle all the
problems that will arise. I feel
good – physically – mentally –
emotionally."
If you repeat these phrases and
meditate on them you can
change the character of your
day by starting off with a
positive frame of mind.

Your attitude will improve
when you act the part of a
happy confident person —
laugh, sing and smile.
Do this for five minutes
every day.

Enthusiasm, energy and determination are essential ingredients to progress. Set goals - give yourself something to aim for. Set your sights high – but be realistic.

Success is the next step
– past failure.

Your attitude affects how
you feel physically and
mentally and affects how
successful you are in
achieving your goals.

Your attitude should always
be the same whoever you are
with – always be
positive and helpful.

A positive attitude
always wins the day. What
you give out will return to
you multiplied.

Negative thoughts:
The feeling of confidence
you have depends on the type
of thoughts which habitually
occupy your mind. If you
constantly fix your mind on
negative events that might
happen – you will constantly
feel insecure and unhappy.
As you think –
so shall you be.

Positive thoughts:
Confidence and happiness are
what you want, flash out all
your old worn out thoughts
and fill your mind with fresh
new creative ones – of faith,
love and goodness.

Positive attitudes are
developed - start developing
yours today.

Take Pride In Who You Are

When you are looking for success and happiness, you must believe in yourself and have faith in your own abilities. For a life which is full of joy and achievement, you must have confidence in your own powers.

The way you behave
is a reflection
of your character.

Smile:
A friendly smile gets
everyone off to a good start
– be cheerful even though
you may not feel like it. Have
a sense of humour – don't
take yourself too seriously,
sometimes a little humour
can put everything in
perspective.

Learn to depend on yourself
that doesn't mean being
selfish, it means taking
responsibility for yourself.

Most of our unhappiness
keeps us living in the past and
prevents us fully living in the
present.

Never take counsel of your
fears, they can create stress
and unhappiness.

Praise yourself when
you deserve it,
be kind to yourself.

Learn to address
and deal with what
makes you stressful.
Take time out to
reflect on
necessary changes.

Trust yourself and
your perceptions
– have confidence
in your abilities.

Learn to listen to
your inner voice
– it will guide you.

Learn To
Welcome Changes

Experiment with new ideas,
be flexible. Cultivate a sense
of humour - don't take life so
seriously – have fun.

Take time out to
reflect on where
you want your life
to go, then make
it happen - with
the right attitude.

You must close
doors before you
can open new ones.

Don't opt out
when things
become tough,
it's never
too late to
make changes.

Learn to accept
and enjoy responsibility.
Commitment has its rewards.

Change your life
by changing the
way you think.

You're the one with
the power to
change your life
— start now.

Winners
And
Losers

– Which One
Are You?

Characteristics
of Winners, they have:
A presence, charisma,
enthusiasm, they look and
feel confident, are always well
turned out and have a
positive attitude.

Remember your
attitude to a problem
determines the end
result. Whatever you
do success depends
on your attitude.
A positive attitude
always wins.

Learn about independence.
A true winner
depends on
his own power.

Tenacity: winners
succeed when
the going gets tough.

Winners have Oomph!!
They have
'get up and go'.

To be successful you
must be a winner and be
positive. Qualifications are a
bonus. Winners take special
care of others by providing
outstanding personal service.
Take time to consider
others, this attitude
marks a true winner.

The secret of good relations is to adopt the same attitude with everyone you meet: a winning attitude.

The first step
to a winning
attitude starts
with you.

Share Yourself
With Others

Bring love and light
to others. It not only
brightens their day
but also yours.

Share problems by
communicating
– a problem shared
is the first step to resolving it.

Take time to be
with others and
to share thoughts
– relaxation
is heaven sent.

Make a mental
note to praise
when someone
deserves it.

Make someone
happy every day.

Be thoughtful
in your actions,
it costs you nothing.

Learn something
from others by
listening and be
sincerely interested
in them – in their
point of view.

Think before you act.
A few moments
thought can save
embarrassment.

Learn to co-operate
with others to achieve
common goals.

A positive attitude is infectious. Spend time with people who feel good about themselves. Self-esteem affects your attitude.

Learn to distance
yourself from
negative thinking
people – their presence will
affect your performance.

Be dependable -
dependability is
important to
efficiency and
success in your life.

Charm your way to success -
the most successful people
are charming.

Learn to treat
people with respect,
no matter what the problem
or situation. Show people
that you respect them,
everyone wants
and deserves respect.

Treating others with
respect can make getting
things done easier and more
pleasant for everyone.

Positive action:
Courtesy – Kindness
– Tenderness – Love.

Negative action:
Discourtesy – Unkindness –
Cruelty – Hate.

Learn to develop love
and understanding
for those around you – you
don't have to
agree with them,
you just have to
try to understand them.

Show you care,
it can make
someone feel special.

Give something
of yourself,
even if it's just a compliment
– it will make
someone feel happy.

Value others' opinions,
one is not always right.

Try not to be dogmatic
in your approach,
no-one likes a bully!

Learn to be of
service to others,
take time out
to help them.

Take the initiative
to help, many hands
make light work.

Do not criticise others,
no-one likes criticism
– everyone needs attention,
admiration and affection
– in large doses!

When someone
appears angry
with you send
them love.

Show others how
the right attitude
can change their lives.

Man thrives when
he feels that
he is successful
in being there
for others.

Be Courteous

Courtesy is good
manners. Courteous people
are polite, interested,
understanding,
helpful, pleasant
and sincere.

Courtesy begins with a
positive attitude
– thinking positively
is the first step to
creating more in your life –
and getting more out of it.
Believe in yourself recognise
your strengths and abilities.

To be courteous
means following
the golden rule.
Treat others the
way you would
like to be treated
yourself. You will
find that most people
will return your
courtesy and respect.

Take time to
help others be
successful, one
day someone
will help you.

Courtesy is
consideration for
others – what you
say and do
– "Please"
– "Thank you"
– "May I?"
– "Do you mind?"

Courtesy is good
manners and
makes you
feel GOOD.

Courtesy means
being punctual in
keeping time and dates.
No one likes to be
kept waiting. Being
punctual shows
consideration for
other people.

Courtesy means
being sincerely
interested in the other
person – courtesy costs
nothing, but is
worth everything:
"How are you?"
"How is your family?"

Courtesy means be patient
and listen to the other person
even if you are not
particularly interested.
Communicate clearly so that
others understand you –
and be sincere.
It is easy to be sincere in
what you say and do.

Listen carefully to
others. Courtesy
means good communication
– develop the habit of
keeping each other
informed of where
you are and what
you are doing.

You can develop serenity and quiet attitudes through your conversation. The words we use and the tone in which we use them — we can talk ourselves into being nervous, highly strung and upset. We can also achieve quiet reactions. Talk peacefully to be peaceful.

Being pleasant
doesn't cost anything
– it just makes
you more friends.

Success is about
being courteous,
thoughtful and caring.
Try it!

If and when people ignore
you, send them love and
always be pleasant.

"Sorry".
A word that
breaks down barriers.

Start practising courtesy,
you'll find it pays
instant dividends – gives you
ease and poise, prevents
friction with others, speeds
action towards your goals and
makes you FEEL GOOD!

Balance Your Life

Recreation. Enjoy
yourself – plan leisure time,
set aside time for personal
recreation. Take time to find
out what is and what's not
important in your life.

Make time for hobbies.
All the great people
in life have hobbies.

Take responsibility
to create new interests.

He Who Plants Kindness Gathers Love

Always remember: what you give out, money, love or service always comes back multiplied but not necessarily from the same source that it was given.

What goes around
comes around
– what you sow,
so shall you reap.

Give the world
the best you have
and the best will
come back to you.

The only safe
and sure way
to destroy an
enemy is to make
them your friend.

Take responsibility
for your actions.
Remember – what you give
out comes back multiplied.

Try reflecting on the following verse:
When there's righteousness in the heart
There's beauty in the character
When there's beauty in the character
There's harmony in the home
When there's harmony in the home
There's order in the nation
When there's order in each nation
There's PEACE in the World

Chinese Proverb

A little about Rosie and her vision

I have been working with individuals and groups for the past ten years offering self-awareness and guidance. I am a trained Stress Management Consultant, Counsellor, Reflexologist, Spiritual Advisor and Speaker.

I believe that we all play a part in the overall plan of shaping our country and world to become a place for everyone to enjoy and be proud of and for this to happen we need as individuals to take responsibility for ourselves and our lives to create, good health, happiness, success and harmony.

Currently undertaking a Masters Degree at The University of Brighton in Change Management. My idea is to link my background with structuring a new programme of taking Spirituality into Organisations via self-awareness presentations, consultations, and on-site therapy for stress-relief and relaxation.

For information on one to one consultations presentations and training please contact:

Hamilton McGinty
Personal Development Consultants
2 Aldingbourne House
Aldingbourne Drive
Crockerhill
Chichester
West Sussex
PO18 OLG

Telephone/Fax: 01243 545268
E Mail: rhamiltonm@AOL.com